50 THINGS BOOK SERIES REVIEWS FROM READERS

I recently downloaded a couple of books from this series to read over the weekend thinking I would read just one or two. However, I so loved the books that I read all the six books I had downloaded in one go and ended up downloading a few more today. Written by different authors, the books offer practical advice on how you can perform or achieve certain goals in life, which in this case is how to have a better life.

The information is simple to digest and learn from, and is incredibly useful. There are also resources listed at the end of the book that you can use to get more information.

50 Things To Know To Have A Better Life: Self-Improvement Made Easy! by Dannii Cohen

---

This book is very helpful and provides simple tips on how to improve your everyday life. I found it to be useful in improving my overall attitude.

50 Things to Know For Your Mindfulness & Meditation Journey by Nina Edmondso

---

Quick read with 50 short and easy tips for what to think about before starting to homeschool.

50 Things to Know About Getting Started with Homeschool by Amanda Walton

I really enjoyed the voice of the narrator, she speaks in a soothing tone. The book is a really great reminder of things we might have known we could do during stressful times, but forgot over the years.

- HarmonyHawaii

50 Things to Know to Manage Your Stress: Relieve The Pressure and Return The Joy To Your Life

by Diane Whitbeck

There is so much waste in our society today. Everyone should be forced to read this book. I know I am passing it on to my family.

50 Things to Know to Downsize Your Life: How To Downsize, Organize, And Get Back to Basics

by Lisa Rusczyk Ed. D.

Great book to get you motivated and understand why you may be losing motivation. Great for that person who wants to start getting healthy, or just for you when you need motivation while having an established workout routine.

50 Things To Know To Stick With A Workout: Motivational Tips To Start The New You Today

by Sarah Hughes

50 THINGS TO KNOW ABOUT PTSD

YOU DON'T HAVE TO SUFFER ALONE

By: Amanda D'Aquila

50 Things to Know About PTSD Copyright © 2019 by CZYK Publishing LLC. All Rights Reserved.

All rights reserved. No part of this book may be reproduced in any form or by any electronic or mechanical means including information storage and retrieval systems, without permission in writing from the author. The only exception is by a reviewer, who may quote short excerpts in a review.

The statements in this book are of the authors and may not be the views of CZYK Publishing or 50 Things to Know.

Cover designed by: Ivana Stamenkovic
Cover Image: https://pixabay.com/en/man-sitting-back-looking-view-690201/

CZYK Publishing Since 2011.

50 Things to Know
Visit our website at www.50thingstoknow..com

Lock Haven, PA
All rights reserved.
ISBN: 9781793852045

50 THINGS TO KNOW ABOUT PTSD

BOOK DESCRIPTION

What is PTSD? How does it affect daily life? Are you a survivor? If you want to find out the answer to these questions, this book is for you.

50 Things to Know about PTSD offers a hands on, informational approach to answer the tough questions most books don't shine light on. Here, is a captivating tribute to those suffering and learning how to cope with someone who has been through it.

This book will teach you the ways of Post Traumatic Stress Disorder and how to live a fulfilling and rewarding life with this illness. Interested? Well, flip the page, and let's get reading.

TABLE OF CONTENTS

50 Things to Know
Book Series
Reviews from Readers
BOOK DESCRIPTION
TABLE OF CONTENTS
DEDICATION
ABOUT THE AUTHOR
INTRODUCTION
1. What Does PTSD Stand For?
2. What Is PTSD?
3. Cause of PTSD
4. Symptoms of PTSD
5. Find More Information
6. How the World Looks to Individuals with PTSD
7. Fear and PTSD
8. Triggers and PTSD
9. What Is a Trigger?
10. Who Gets PTSD?
11. PTSD Stigma
12. "Veterans Only Get PTSD" Is a Myth
13. PTSD Does Not Mean You Are Crazy
14. PTSD Does Not Mean You Are Weak
15. PTSD Does Not Discriminate
16. Can Animals Have PTSD?

17. Can Children Have PTSD?
18. Who's at Risk for PTSD?
19. Is PTSD Contagious?
20. PTSD Is Technically Not Curable
21. Only 50% of People Experiencing PTSD Actually Get Help
22. PTSD Treatment
23. Therapy Treatment
24. Medication Treatment
25. Bottling It in
26. How Long Is Recovery?
27. Symptoms Can Occur Whenever, Wherever
28. PTSD Is NOT as Simple as "Getting Over It"
29. Many Times, PTSD Goes Misdiagnosed
30. PTSD Can Have Many Underlying Diagnoses Caused by This Disorder
31. Women Are More Likely to Get PTSD
32. The Only Way to Experience PTSD, Is by Having It
33. Many People with PTSD, Try Alternative, Negative Coping Skills
34. Negative Coping Skills
35. What Is Abuse?
36. Physical? Emotional? Verbal?
37. Victim?
38. Is PTSD a New "Trend"?

39. How Long Has PTSD Been around?
40. What to Do If Your Family Member/Friend Is Experiencing PTSD Symptoms
41. Getting Help
42. 12 Step
43. 12 Step Meeting to Support Survivors
44. Websites to Connect You with a Trauma Therapists
45. Denial
46. Waterworks
47. Telling Your Friends
48. Letter of Apology Assignment
49. Remember to Breathe
50. Moment of Silence

Other Helpful Resources

50 Things to Know

DEDICATION

This book is dedicated to all those suffering with PTSD, and the individuals who helped me along my journey of recovery. We are warriors.

ABOUT THE AUTHOR

Watch my words unravel. Watch them bend and boil, like the popping of an oil licked pan. Listen to them like chorus on repeat in your ears, let them stay, lingering between your toes. I'll keep you warm like socks. My arms are the flames from a bonfire at brisk, that burn chocolates on Graham crackers.

I am a poet, a writer, and a survivor. My words are my expression and the world is my blank canvas. I have been through the rough, and come out shining. I know you can do the same.

Mandaquila on Medium
https://link.medium.com/eZNh4smwJS

INTRODUCTION

People may view you as damaged goods. As someone too fragile to hold, whose bones are weary and breaking. Although, this may be true, for trauma is painful and hard. But, you are also a warrior, a fighter, and a survivor.

Don't forget the roots of your soul. Plant them in the beautiful world, for you will see them bloom one day.

Be the butterfly, spread your wings, and fly. Open the page, and see how living with a mental disorder is possible. Take me for example!

Your heartbeat begins to escalate. Fainted phantograms race across your eyes, bits of spoiled memories flooding your psyche- you stop in your tracks. Your fingers begin to shake like the moving of hands on a piano, playing a graceful symphony you know far too well. You are alone. Nothing will stop the shaking now, like a storm you have waited to come, with lighting shattering your bones. If you ever have been through a life-altering event, that may have caused you distress or negative symptoms afterwards, you probably went through trauma. This is PTSD. Ever wonder what Post Traumatic Stress Disorder really is? What goes on in the brain, body, and soul when a survivor has gone through a life-altering, traumatic event?

Hopefully, if you are looking for answers somewhere, this guide can aid you in finding them. I myself am a trauma survivor and have made this in the hopes that an individual, even one single person, may benefit from a few words from someone whose been through the rough patches, and come out a warrior. Here are some questions or concerns answered. Here are fifty facts about PTSD.

(Forewarning: Everything varies with every other trauma survivor. My tips may not be helpful to some, but I hope it opens and ignites your mind to think more about PTSD. I do describe my own situation, which may be different than others. Trigger warning: Although my examples aren't very thorough, I do describe some possible traumatic events.)

1. WHAT DOES PTSD STAND FOR?

PTSD stands for Post-Traumatic Stress Disorder. The name itself may sound intimidating to some, but more people actually have the disorder than you may realize. In fact, many people whom you pass on a daily basis, have most likely experienced some traumatic event themselves. The people you pass on a subway, or the millions of people waltzing down Chicago's crowded streets, have a past. They are people just like you. PTSD interferes with the brain, therefore there are many times it goes unnoticed to the human eye. Individuals who experience this pain, may not always show their true fear. Instead of leaning on others for support, they isolate and internalize their feelings as a defensive tactic.

2. WHAT IS PTSD?

My definition of PTSD would be that it is a whole pile of shit. Yes, that is correct, post-traumatic stress disorder is hard, painful, and it truly sucks. It is when an individual witnesses or experiences an incident or event that traumatizes them into a constant state of stress. Each person's stress will look differently depending on how they deal with the trauma. Not every survivor's symptoms are going to be the same as another survivor. There are many different symptoms, many different causes, and with that, thankfully many different treatments.

Many will tell you experiencing a traumatic event, isn't that big of a deal. My apologies society, but you are wrong. I validate the strength and bravery it takes to pursue past the past. It takes courage to fight a battle in which no one else can help you fight, and move forward from it. There is no outside force feeling what you are feeling, except others who have gone through it as well. A good thing to remember, is you are not alone. It may be a man versus man fight, but there is a whole support system of weapons to help individuals move past PTSD. The battle is not over until you win, and I am smelling victory. Let's continue!

3. CAUSE OF PTSD

There are many different ways an individual can get PTSD. There is not only one cause. The cause of someone becoming traumatized is anything in that individual's life that impacted their psyche to the point where they can no longer function due to their PTSD. Examples of an event could be receiving abuse as a child/as an adult, being sexually assaulted, a dysfunctional family, natural disasters, the list goes on and on. It will vary from individual to individual. No one person has the same exact PTSD as another. Society itself contains many traumatic stressors that may be deteriorating to people. Not to worry you, but there aren't many classes out there for parents or

50 Things to Know

individuals to know how to teach the right way to go about life, raising a child, and sex. Like for instance, my trauma was being raped- My abuser was probably never taught not to have sex with an unconscious individual. This is one example of a big problem facing the American educational system! We can teach math and geometry for hours, read a whole book in two weeks, but not teach children the right and wrong ways of life.

A good thing to remember about PTSD is wherever or whomever you receive the trauma from, it is not your fault. It is simply the fault of whoever or whatever caused you to be traumatized. This is a big issue that many PTSD patients fail to realize. They must forgive themselves, for it is not their fault. It took me awhile to realize the rape I encountered was not my fault. PTSD is the voice in the back of your head, telling you to be afraid of the world because of a fearful situation you encountered.

4. SYMPTOMS OF PTSD

I would recommend looking through the symptoms especially if you feel like you may experience PTSD. Symptoms can vary, person to person, some may be more intense, some may be in the back of your brain. The following can last as long as your body and mind need to wrap their head around what happened. From my research, you are diagnosed with this disorder if any of these last a month or more after your traumatic event.:

1. Intrusive flashbacks to the traumatic event that occurred. Flashbacks are re experiencing the trauma again, like dreams in the day time, while your awake. Flashbacks may lead to dissociations. Vivid nightmares regarding your trauma.
2. Dissociation, "zoned out" most of the day, or in your daily activity. Never feeling present in the moment enough to concentrate.
3. Emotional numbness, can't feel the same way you used to. Along with this, life has become unmanageable, cannot get up in the morning.
4. Avoidance of anything related to your trauma for it brings you back to when it happened, and some individuals may push down their trauma and want to not think about it.
5. Feeling jumpy or hypervigilant, anything will scare trauma survivors such as loud noises, sound of something related to their trauma, even a song can send them into a flashback.
6. On the opposite end, may feel a flood of crying spells, panic attacks, etc.

Throughout my findings, these are the most known symptoms of PTSD. If you are experiencing any of these or other symptoms, definitely consult those with your therapist or doctor in order for them to be able to treat you the best way they see fit. Another thing to add, if you are seeking treatment, I definitely recommend complete transparency. The people treating you, although they seem very business oriented, are there to help. It may seem scary at first to be honest and open up, but honesty only leads you closer in recovery.

Here is a great website that broadcasts even more symptoms!
https://adaa.org/understanding-anxiety/posttraumatic-stress-disorder-ptsd/symptoms

5. FIND MORE INFORMATION

https://www.everydayhealth.com/ptsd/guide/resources/

This website has helped me navigate my disorder. There are many specific resources that may help you in learning more about your PTSD. I definitely suggest a first step of getting a therapist. You are then able to unload all your problems out on the table instead of bottling it in, and causing more issues in the future.

6. HOW THE WORLD LOOKS TO INDIVIDUALS WITH PTSD

The world is an abyss of fear and pain. Passion seems so small when every problem seems like the world is crashing down upon your shoulders. For some, life becomes unmanageable, basic daily duties seem impossible. Some have trouble showering, eating, going outside, and even breathing makes you think of the traumatic event that occurred. For myself, I no longer view men in the same way I used to. I am afraid of anyone who puts their hand on me, talks to me, and greets me who is male. That is no insult to men, but due to my trauma that is just how it is until I recover.

 Individuals with trauma must figure how to live with their PTSD. I started self defense classes, bought mace to put on my keys at night, and don't go to public places without a friend. Creating a safe space for yourself in the world that seems scary, is a first step in combating your PTSD.

 It may be hard to realize,but there is so much beauty in the life you are living. My therapist once did an exercise with me, where I closed my eyes and he asked me "Remember a time when you laughed so hard, you cried. A laughter that stems from the belly and makes you want to roll over laughing". After I remembered the memory, I suddenly had a smile the rest of the day. It is hard to realize, but just like the moments from your trauma are in your memory, so are the good times. Happiness is not something we stumble upon, buy, or get rewarded after acts of kindness, it is within us. There are happy times in our daily activities- like a cup of coffee, a cigarette, etc. Whatever it is for you, it will benefit us to reconnect with this part of our brains.

7. FEAR AND PTSD

All individuals with PTSD are fearful of a traumatic event. Although they are most of the time numb to feelings, the truth is their emotional tank is low, because of their lack in ability to be vulnerable due to what happened to them in their past. Fear plays a big role in PTSD, along with hypervigilance and possible flashbacks.

To me, fear was the hardest symptom to get past. Being afraid of the outside world makes things tough to accomplish. I dropped out of school, couldn't keep up with grades, couldn't socialize properly due to my fear of men and people in general. The paranoia is a symptom of PTSD, so the fear you are feeling is valid and real. This fear becomes a shelter for us to rest in, a coping mechanism to stay away from the scary. Combatting this paranoia is like in the Indiana Jones movie, when he has to jump on an invisible bridge. He knows it is there, but he can't see it right now. He has to give up everything that seems real, and stick with his gut. In order to recover, we have to take the leap of faith that treatment is going to help and our doctors and therapists will be there to catch us. It is hard to get over fear, but knowing there is a path of freedom waiting for us to cross, can give us the faith to take the leap.

There is a cure to this fear! I took self defense classes and realized that I am more powerful than my trauma. I am discussing this as if it is easy. Trust me- you have to do the dirty work, and it is going to be tough. There are going to be days where it feels like there is no end in sight. The suffering may feel unbearable, but, believing in yourself and your power is the most important aspect to combat the fear.

8. TRIGGERS AND PTSD

Many things can trigger and individual with PTSD into a flashback or dissociation. Each trigger is specific to each individual. For example, triggers can seem miniscule like a certain song playing at a coffee shop, but it makes a big aspect to a person who had that song playing during their trauma experience.

Learning your triggers is a great next step in learning to live with PTSD. Once you know them, you are able to format a safety plan if those occur during your day. For me, a trigger is strangers going up to me and greeting me. I use mindfulness, breathing techniques, and riding the wave DBT skills to combat this.

I greatly recommend researching what DBT skills would work in your crisis plan!

9. WHAT IS A TRIGGER?

A trigger is anything that leads an individual into remembering or re experiencing their traumatic event. For veterans, snow blowers and lawnmowers may be triggering for the sound is similar to the rumbling of a bomb or gunshot. Each trigger is different to each person. To know if you are triggering an individual who has PTSD, feel free to ask them if they are able to share their triggers so you know what to say and what not to say. This will guarantee a good relationship with the person with PTSD.

10. WHO GETS PTSD?

PTSD does not discriminate. No one race, sex, background, class is subject to PTSD, it is all relative to if you have experienced a traumatic experience and are impacted by it with the symptoms that apply to the disorder.

Unfortunately, there is no road map to your life that will let you know beforehand if you will get PTSD. Unlike some theories with depression, anxiety, etc. about the illnesses having a line in families, PTSD is a bit different. Although, usually if a family's parents experienced abuse or had a dysfunctional family growing up, they will sometimes act the same because it is all they know. If a boy grew up with an abusive father, then turned abusive and didn't get help or have empathy, most likely he will abuse his child and that child may be at risk for PTSD. If your family, friend, parner, or loved one is abusive, you have a higher risk of having PTSD.

But, it is all relative. Some individuals receive traumatic experienced differently than others. If one individual is in shock after a car accident, and the other is not, from my research, there is no reason behind why. All there is is how your brain receives trauma. It is possible for two people to experience a life-altering, negative event, and only one of them to get PTSD. It all is determined by how your body and mind react to the situation.

11. PTSD STIGMA

PTSD has many big stigmas attached to the disorder that society has created. This is a big reason why many individuals don't get diagnosed properly and don't seek out treatment. They are too afraid of how their friends, family, and social media will feel if they admit to having a mental illness.

I wanted to touch on the fact that the negative stigmas you might hear from your friends or family, are wrong. Society creates these lies that individuals with mental illness are "weak" or "making it up", but that is actually the opposite. We are the ones who have the strength and courage to fight back the stigmas, and get help for our disorders. Everyone with mental illness, is a warrior. They have destroyed their demons on their own, admitted that their life being unmanageable, and experiencing a self awareness that is unlike the people without it. If you are without a mental illness, please treat us survivors with respect. We have been through rock bottom, and got up shining.

12. "VETERANS ONLY GET PTSD" IS A MYTH

Many people associate PTSD with war heros or veterans. The movies featuring PTSD are mostly all in regards to veterans not being able to come home and manage their life successfully due to their disorder. Although, anyone who experiences a traumatic event has the chance of getting PTSD. It is not just solely veterans, although many soldiers who come home from war experience it as well. Take me for example, I got PTSD and I am not a veteran.

Veterans do though have a higher chance of coming home with PTSD. Your sprinkler sounds like bullets ricocheting off walls and human flesh. You jump at loud noises like tea heating and when the toaster bings. Nightmares flood your dreams of past times, makes you wake up sweating and hyperventilating. These are all symptoms of PTSD. Although these are more specific to a veteran, someone not involved in war can still obtain these. There is much more awareness about PTSD going around now a days, which is very uplifting to know you are not alone in your disorders.

13. PTSD DOES NOT MEAN YOU ARE CRAZY

Listen up, all who believe they are going crazy, experiencing symptoms that feel like their life is crashing down and daily activities have become unmanageable- it is all normal to feel what you are feeling. Mental illness, although there is a lot more awareness now, has a stigma that individuals who are experiencing any disorder, are crazy. That is simply not the truth. Rough experiences lead to rough patches. Healing and recovery is not linear, many must jump through a variety of obstacles to get to the freedom of a powerful mind. It is not an overnight process, so feeling stressed is normal. But, the good thing is you are able to have an amazing treatment team that is on your side throughout it, to lean on and process, to love you for exactly who you are. It is also good to remember that the suffering can slowly dissolve into a memory one day. Stay hopeful, keep your head up, and remember you are not crazy.

14. PTSD DOES NOT MEAN YOU ARE WEAK

PTSD actually is the opposite, for you are a survivor of a very traumatic experience that altered your life. You made it past the difficult part and you are still alive, reading this article right now. The fact that you are trying to read more about your disorder and getting help is so incredibly strong. Remember that you are a survivor, and you've already won the first fight, now is the battle. It is hard, because PTSD makes you feel inferior, makes you feel like the weight on your shoulder is overwhelmingly impossible to get through, but the truth is you are so powerful. Processing is hard, getting up in the morning is hard, and making it through one day at a time is hard, but guess what- you are here doing it. Getting through all the pain that was inflicted on you, patching up your wounds, and actually healing. Recovery is a path of many difficulties and struggles, but you are strong enough to get through it- I promise.

15. PTSD DOES NOT DISCRIMINATE

Mentioned earlier in the article, there is not one type of individual who can get PTSD. It is simply about your brain and body figuring out how to deal with the amount of stress inflicted on you from the event. But, this means you are also not alone. It is possible the person sitting next to you on the subway train is struggling with the same disorder. It was not until I went to a treatment center that I realized how big the trauma community is, and how encouraging it is to have friends who have gone through similar or related events. It is also inspiring to know that people, many people, are in recovery, staying strong, building a life from themselves after a PTSD diagnosis. It definitely takes a toll on millions of lives across the nation, but just remember to hold your head high and keep preserving, the fight is not over, the battle may not be won, but have faith in yourself and your high power to guide you through the obstacles and challenges along the way. Know that you have a support system that's got your back- even me!

16. CAN ANIMALS HAVE PTSD?

There are many animals who have experienced some sort of abuse or traumatic experience that greatly affects their day to day lives. Some are so frightened after being mistreated, that they are prescribed meds just like you. This is in any animal, whether it be a cow, dog, or pig. The fact is, they have ways to improve their quality of life after that has happened, and so do you! With a treatment team that challenges you to get back to the things you were passionate about, slowly and at your own pace, life day to day will get simpler everyday.

17. CAN CHILDREN HAVE PTSD?

Many people I was in treatment at one point in my journey, were younger than 12. There is no age limit or timeline for people. Unfortunately, most of the time many individuals experience abuse or neglect as a child that could put them at risk for having PTSD. That is why there is adolescent or child therapy out there, for those struggling at a young age. If you are a parent reading this, and your child is experiencing many of the symptoms listed, I definitely suggest connecting your little person with a therapist that specializes in trauma. There are so many out there, and the sooner the treatment, the sooner recovery is possible. The longer you wait, the easier it is for them to bottle their experiences inside, which is a very unhealthy coping skill.

18. WHO'S AT RISK FOR PTSD?

Unfortunately, there is no list for who is at risk. Although, the individuals who may be at risk will be whoever has experienced a traumatic event. Traumatic events can vary from person to person, and the way individuals receive the trauma and how their mind decides to process it all. Nobody can choose if they have PTSD or not, it is inflicted on them from the past experience.

19. IS PTSD CONTAGIOUS?

Obvious answer, but no. What is contagious is common stressors society is putting on individuals these days and the lack of education about mental illness and activities that improve the mood and a child's way to cope properly and know what is right and wrong.

For example, some parents may not know it is not a great way to discipline your child by hitting them. And, children who have received this treatment in their childhood, don't know that that is the wrong way, and that they don't deserve the abuse they are receiving. This is the same with sexual abuse as a child, and many more incidents.

Truth is, the education system should show children how to treat others, and how they deserve to be treated- in a kind, positive, and overall accepting community.

20. PTSD IS TECHNICALLY NOT CURABLE

Okay, hear me out. There is not a definite cure to PTSD, not one way to solve each individual's pain. There is not one treatment plan that comes in line with everyone. There is also not one medication that can solve and make you forget what was inflicted on you.

There are coping skills, medications, and activities that may minimize your symptoms of PTSD, so life is easier to manage and each day will get easier, and be a projection towards recovery. But, not going to lie here, there are always going to be bad days. Always going to be days where your mind will recount the experience you were involved in. The silverlining is, in treatment, you will learn DBT skills and different positive coping skills to get through the hard times. Healing is not linear, there are ups and downs, lefts and rights, but the good thing to remember is there is always a light at the end of the tunnel. A reason to move forward, even after taking steps backwards sometimes. Don't forget how strong you are and how far you have come.

21. ONLY 50% OF PEOPLE EXPERIENCING PTSD ACTUALLY GET HELP

Yes, there are people roaming the streets who are dealing with similar symptoms that you are, but not getting treatment. They go about their lives, solving their problems with negative coping skills and bad habits.

The best way to solve this and encourage someone to get help, is spreading awareness of the disorder. Many individuals may not realize what Post-traumatic Stress Disorder is, or ways to help them with their symptoms from the experience they had. Spreading awareness involves sharing articles, reading brochures, and donating to different organizations that help trauma patients. Help is there, right at your fingertips, the best thing for a life in recovery is grasping treatment with both hands and being as translucent as possible to the people in your support system. You got this, stay strong.

22. PTSD TREATMENT

There are many different PTSD treatments out there. Holistic approaches, solely medication, DBT skills, the list goes on. Research about what treatment you think is best for your case. Also, keep reading to find out more!

23. THERAPY TREATMENT

You walk into the office, there is a stranger you don't know, asking you very personal questions- that is scary. The fear of therapy is real and many individuals out there do not go because of that. Or maybe they have tried it out once, and didn't personally like it.

I recommend researching about the therapist you are going to receive treatment from. There are many different therapists out there, music therapists, art therapists, and therapists specializing in trauma. For me, I had to go to four different therapists before I felt comfortable with one.

Furthermore, the first session is always the hardest. Many therapists recommend you trying it out for three sessions before going somewhere else. A lot of what the first session entails is background information. But, once you get past the hard part, processing and being translucent is possible.

Also, if you feel as though once a week therapy is not enough, there are facilities out there which specialize in treating multiple disorders, including ones that are solely trauma based. Here you get to meet individuals who are going through similar struggles as you are, and building friendships and relationships with such an encouraging community is really beneficial. I have gone to many treatment facilities, until I felt confident in my recovery. Again, treatment is not linear, there are going to be bumps in the road, individuals and therapists you might not connect with, but keep working and don't give up! Recovery is there and possible, it just may take some digging to find what helps you the most.

24. MEDICATION TREATMENT

Here is the where a stigma that might kick in. When an individual struggles with a trauma event, it could change their brain chemistry. This is shown through their specific symptoms. Sometimes, the brain cannot go through such a triggering experience on its own. Just like you having to go through therapy, sometimes your brain needs a hand to hold or a push to get you back on the right track. Many look down upon medication, some people believe individuals become reliant on the drugs or it changes their behavior.

Although medication does have many side effects most of the time, which I do encourage you to look into, sometimes it is necessary for recovery. For me, my brain had dropped into the biggest depression, I felt suicidal and couldn't get out of my bed every morning, so I found medication that helped me with nightmares, insomnia, and depression.

If you believe you need medication to help you along your path, it is normal. PTSD medications are out there for a reason. To start, find a psychiatrist. Get a recommendation from your insurance, therapist, or friends who may be on mental illness medications. Before you start taking a medication, I definitely recommend researching about it, the side effects, and how it can benefit you and your recovery. It is your journey and you are able to decide what you believe to be right for you. So take action and don't be afraid or doubt your gut feeling. If you believe you need medication, go for it.

25. BOTTLING IT IN

Attention! The fear of talking about your trauma is real. Remember though, processing what happened is really beneficial. If you push your struggles and issues down, it will only prolong your suffering. I definitely recommend finding someone willing to just listen to what happened. I was afraid for a whole year and a half before I talked about what happened. I pushed it down, deep in my soul, and let it eat at parts of my identity. I was fearful of what people may think or treat me afterwards. But, I can tell you, it is so freeing to talk about it. It puts the power back into your hands. Processing is a big step in recovery, try not to be afraid, and talk about it! I promise, it will only benefit your present and future.

26. HOW LONG IS RECOVERY?

Recovery takes as long as your brain, body, and soul need it. A good rule of thumb, is however long ago the trauma happened and however long you kept it a secret, is as long as it takes. But, it varies for each individual. Some people have additionally diagnoses attached to their trauma, some people may need less intense treatment.

If you are fearful of how long it will take, don't be. Think about how long life is and if you want to be living that in stress and constant suffering. After treatment, many people feel reborn. If your life is unmanageable, or even if you are able to manage but with bad habits and negative coping skills, I suggest getting help as soon as you feel comfortable with sharing your experience. There is a light at the end of the tunnel that may feel dark right now. One step at a time, recovery becomes more and more possible. A happy life is more possible with recovery and treatment.

27. SYMPTOMS CAN OCCUR WHENEVER, WHEREVER

You are at a job interview and someone is wearing the same cologne your abuser did. You are at Walmart and a song comes on. You are alone, your mind spiraling. Unfortunately, PTSD symptoms do not choose when to occur. There is not a mental check mark to tell you that you are about to disassociate or go into a flashback, it will slowly creep into your brain with no warning.

On the positive note, taking time to work on your symptoms and become more aware of your warning signs or triggers that occur during an episode, may greatly improve you combatting your symptoms.

28. PTSD IS NOT AS SIMPLE AS "GETTING OVER IT"

If anyone tells you to get over it, don't listen. It is NOT that easy. A traumatic event is called traumatic for a reason- that means it has impacted your brain, soul, and body so much that there is a whole disorder revolved around it. Mental illness as a whole is not possible to just get over. It could take years to process, receive treatment, and finally be okay with what happened.

"Being okay" still doesn't mean the suffering is ending. There are bad days, even in recovery. But, they will be more manageable as treatment gives you the weapons to battle those hardships, and persevere!

29. MANY TIMES, PTSD GOES MISDIAGNOSED

A good analogy one therapist once described to me, is that PTSD is like a big cloud in a rainstorm. It is the creator of tiny raindrops, but all is relative and involved in a gloomy day. The big cloud is PTSD, but there are diagnoses that go under trauma. When an individual has PTSD, they may experience symptoms from a mood disorder, personality disorder, depression, anxiety, etc. You can be diagnosed with many of these things, but not PTSD, even though you have been through something traumatic.

I wasn't diagnosed with PTSD for awhile. I wouldn't talk about my trauma or symptoms, therefore I was only diagnosed with anxiety, depression, and an eating disorder. But, I know now that those were only raindrops. The big cloud above me was my PTSD, and once I processed that and gained control of my life, I was able to work on the other issues I was facing. The sun was finally revealed to me and recovery is possible.

30. PTSD CAN HAVE MANY UNDERLYING DIAGNOSES CAUSED BY THIS DISORDER

Like I stated earlier, PTSD is the big umbrella that has many underlying illnesses. You may experience depression, anxiety, eating disorders, addiction, etc. from PTSD. This does not make you less strong, it just means your journey has been a tough one, and for you to gain control and for your brain to wrap around what happened to you, many diagnoses can pile up on top of you. But, the good thing is, there is treatment for all these. There are ways you can feel happy waking up in the morning, at a meal, or not using. Recovery is not one straight line, but has many paths and obstacles you encounter in order to get at the light of the tunnel. If you get diagnosed with more illnesses that you expected, don't be afraid, for there is support for each and every illness out there. Keep working hard and remember you are not crazy. What is crazy, is the trauma inflicted on you that should have not happened, and is not your fault in the slightest.

31. WOMEN ARE MORE LIKELY TO GET PTSD

Yes, throughout my research, I found women are more likely to get PTSD. I believe, as a woman with PTSD, that us females out there have been getting the bad side of the bargain. But, good to know, that we are all so much stronger than what happened to us. We have risen, and we will rise again, stronger. We are here to win the battle over this disorder, and live a happy, content life without our past leaving lifelong scars. So, let's do this!

32. THE ONLY WAY TO EXPERIENCE PTSD, IS BY HAVING IT

For those who have loved ones with PTSD, it may be hard to wrap your mind around all this. If your loved one experiences any of the symptoms, it could be frightening if you don't have post traumatic stress disorder. But, please know they are not making it up.

Everything going through their mind is real- the possible nightmares, flashbacks, mood changes, etc. could all be because of an event that occurred in their life. Coping with PTSD is hard, it is a pile of rocks landing on top of you that is extremely overwhelming, so if your loved one needs time to process and cope, allow them this. Validate their suffering, validate what they are going through. Just having someone on their side who knows what they are going through is real, is a huge benefit to anyone with the disorder. Support is extremely important, so remember to not deny them the shoulder or hand they might need.

33. MANY PEOPLE WITH PTSD, TRY ALTERNATIVE, NEGATIVE COPING SKILLS

Negative coping skills are probably the most common reaction after a traumatic event. A negative coping skill is anything they do that is not beneficial to their safety or recovery that they involve themselves in just to cope with all the stress. They can all be secretly sabotaging your well being!

34. NEGATIVE COPING SKILLS

There are many negative coping skills out there. I've listed a few below. Take a look, being aware of how negative each may be on your body and mind could help in making your journey directed towards recovery, not the grave:

- Abusing drugs
- Eating disorders
- Negative self-talk
- Denial
- Placing blame on yourself
- Pushing it down, not talking about it
- Fake happiness
- Wallowing
- Isolating

The list can continue. Treatment helps you with all these. Realizing that your symptoms, can be happening because of negative coping skills. For example, marijuana may make someone feel less motivated, especially if they already have depression. A good start is trying to minimize your negative coping skills. Truth is, it is probably just sabotaging your life even more, so it is harder to get out of rough patches. But a good tip to help you towards adjusting your recovery, is googling some DBT skills and positive ways to cope! Anything to steer you away from making your day to day worse, is always a step in the right direction.

35. WHAT IS ABUSE?

Whether it be from your father, angrily throwing old rum glasses at walls, or your partner, screaming about how he will end his life and yours if you leave him, abuse has many sneaky ways in showing up in our lives. Abuse usually results in post traumatic stress. A traumatic event is what causes this disorder, and boy, abuse is a hell of a traumatic event. I am touching on this to spread awareness on abuse, for the people facing abuse and abusers to realize what is right and wrong.

36. PHYSICAL? EMOTIONAL? VERBAL?

All different abuse can come from anyone. Even if the abuser is a good person, abuse is wrong no matter who does it.

Physical abuse is physically hurting or endangering you, making the environment unsafe. This can be anything, sexual abuse, pushing, punching, leaving bruises or scars on your body. This is completely unacceptable: if you are in an abusive relationship or family, please find a way out. If you cannot, call the abuse hotline to help you, or please tell any individual. No matter how much the abuser manipulates you, how many apologies they may give you, this is wrong, and not acceptable to hurt someone so much.

Emotional abuse and verbal abuse is very hard to detect, for it has a lot to do with manipulation. If you are sad, depressed, or hurt by someone emotionally abusing you, don't hesitate to call the hotline or tell an individual. An example could be demeaning words, making you feel worthless and inferior, diminish your identity, any psychological way an individual may try to demean you through words, or other ways, that leave you feeling at fault or hurt. They could be building you up, only to tear you down vertebrae by vertebrae.

Any abuse is unacceptable. I am including the Domestic Abuse website that can help you navigate what abuse is and how to get out of the unhealthy and very unsafe environment or relationship.

Website: https://www.thehotline.org
Hotline: 1-800-799-SAFE(7233)

37. VICTIM?

Any result of PTSD does not make you a victim. It makes you a survivor. You have survived an event that caused so much stress, that it resulted in emotional and physical trauma.

For me, it was good to remember how many individuals out there had gone through similar situations that I could confide and talk with. It made me feel less alone in the big, scary world.

Labeling yourself as victim may make you feel like you lost a battle. But, it is in fact the opposite. You fought so hard, through a great deal of stressors, and you are still standing here today. That is a result that you are a survivor. Your journey is not over and you are for sure not powerless over the traumatic event. You, or your loved one, is not a victim. The term "victim" makes it seem like you are inferior to your abuser/the event that shaped your trauma. Your trauma may be only a small event in your past, but it does have power over you- just not until you remember how powerful you are. You are so much more than a victim. You survived what happened to you. And not only did you survive, but you are reading this article, trying to find more about what affects your trauma has on you. Researching more about any mental illness you may have, is rewarding for your next steps in recovery. It takes will power to radically accept what happened- you may never accept it, and that's okay. But, the bravery you have to commit to getting help is what makes you a warrior. Destroying your own demons leads to a path of greater determination and success. So, pat yourself on your back! For not only are you not alone, but you have bravery and will power inside of you that radiates. Remember that you are a warrior. And you got this!

38. IS PTSD A NEW "TREND"?

PTSD is finally becoming more prominent in society, but not because it is a "trend". PTSD has been around for a long time, but individuals are feeling more able to talk about it. Before, it was a lot of hiding and bottling in. In the old days, families swept abuse under the rug, leaving everything up in the air and stressors to fall upon the shoulders of the survivors. It is not a new trend, it has always been around.

39. HOW LONG HAS PTSD BEEN AROUND?

PTSD has been around for as many years as traumatic events have been around, it only became a name in the 90s. Many individuals hid their PTSD from the world, but with the community of affected individuals becomes bigger, so does the people feeling more able to talk about it. Society's stigmas have become less and empowerment and encouragement have become more prominent in the 21st century.

40. WHAT TO DO IF YOUR FAMILY MEMBER/FRIEND IS EXPERIENCING PTSD SYMPTOMS

Number one- validate their trauma happened. Many people experiencing PTSD have hard time talking to others about their experience in the first place, so letting them know that you are there for them, and that you believe them is very important. Next, let them go into recovery at their pace. Many individuals have a hard time with regaining power back when they've experienced a traumatic event. Allowing them to be empowered again and reborn is also something to keep in mind. They probably feel alone, so stick by their side. Remember that whatever mood they are in or what symptom they might experience, may be them projecting their pain onto you. Forgive them when this happens and stay by their side. Be an ear to talk to, or a shoulder to cry on. In my recovery, it was very beneficial that my parents were okay with me not calling them as much. As long as they are safe, let them do what they need to find a way to live with what they've experienced. If they are doing something negative, read about what an intervention is. Don't force upon them treatment if they are not ready to face their trauma. Many things can be triggering, so if they are in recovery, ask them what to say and what not to. It is very important to be a good team player, and stick to the sidelines, let them win their battle on their own.

41. GETTING HELP

There are many ways to get help for PTSD. Treatment can be intense, or less intense depending on what each individual needs. Therapy is a good place to start, allowing yourself to talk about what happened can help you feel free and like a weight has been lifted off your shoulders. If you need more treatment for your trauma, medication and residential facilities is a great next step. Medication is very helpful for symptoms. At residential facilities, there are professionals to aid you in your recovery and help you make good decisions during a very sensitive time in your life.

42. 12 STEP

12 step meetings are not just AA or NA! There are communities out there that help encourage you along your journey. The 12 Steps specifically can be not only for alcohol, but you are able to replace that with any disorder. For example, I am going to 12 Step meetings for my mental illnesses, my eating disorders, and other negative coping skills. Keep in mind the options you have to encourage you along your rough days.

Many 12 Steps suggest you try out different groups and go to them at least six times to really give them a chance. One meeting could connect with you more than another. Find a place you feel comfortable! Don't worry, you don't have to speak until you want to. Everyone is very inviting to newcomers.

43. 12 STEP MEETING TO SUPPORT SURVIVORS

There are 12 Step Meetings for survivors of trauma! Below I've attached some links to websites to aid you in this process:

- http://www.naasca.org/Trauma-12Step/

- http://sasaworldwide.org

- https://www.rainn.org/about-national-sexual-assault-telephone-hotline

It is really difficult to go through these tough, painful times alone. That is why it is most important that you seek out support. This will aid you in not internalizing what happened to you, and bottling it all in. If you don't unravel what happened, you may use negative coping skills to deal with the pain. This is why I've attached these awesome websites and resources to help you get connected!

44. WEBSITES TO CONNECT YOU WITH A TRAUMA THERAPISTS

A great, free website to find a therapist or psychiatrist is PsychologyToday.com! You can filter for trauma survivors, your own insurance, and your location. I found my therapist who I've been seeing for years and helped me through my PTSD.

45. DENIAL

Like the stages of grief, there may be stages to your PTSD. For me, I had a hard time accepting that I was a trauma survivor. I thought I could cope, on my own, no matter if my life had become unmanageable. If you are in denial about your trauma, it is okay. People take the steps towards recovery in different ways. Healing is not one straight line, there are many obstacles, like denial, that can stand in your way. But, let me tell you something- whatever happened, it is not your fault. No matter what it was, no one deserves a traumatic event to inflict stress and pain on them. And, you are not alone.

46. WATERWORKS

Many individuals become emotionally numb after experiencing a traumatic event. This is okay, but also keep in mind, no matter what others may say, it is alright to cry. For awhile, I kept my crying to myself. I was embarrassed of being vulnerable in front of people, or even admitting my suffering. Some may put on a happy mask, but it is okay to not be okay. Traumatic events are heavy, tough situations, that require a lot of treatment. Crying may take time, but the wall can break down, and your emotions are allowed to run free. You are allowed to be angry, resentful, pissed off, and sad! Every emotion is valid!

47. TELLING YOUR FRIENDS

It is your story, so you have the ability to choose who you feel you want to share your experience with. I thought I had to tell each friend or person I have ever had an encounter with. But, you don't have to. A big issue that many individuals have is when they have to ask there work for time off due to their disorder. Keep as much information in the sharing as you feel you want to share- no one is entitled to know your story. Remember that you don't need your friends or coworkers validation to know you have PTSD. Stay strong while doing this- retelling your entire story can be very emotionally draining. The more information you share, the more closed off you may be after. Keep it at whatever length you so choose and don't forget that you are in complete control.

48. LETTER OF APOLOGY ASSIGNMENT

Here is a homework assignment to anyone who is going through a traumatic event, or even someone who isn't. Write a letter to yourself, from the perspective of someone you want an apology from. For example, when I did this project, I wrote a letter from my rapist. Many of my friends wrote letters from their parents for not believing them, or if they had abusive parents. Anyone who you have always wanted an apology from but never received one. Remember, you have the right to feel your emotions. If you are extremely mad or sad, sit with that emotion. Allow it to make you feel something. The fact of the matter is, whomever you are "receiving" the letter from, you probably deserve that apology, but you didn't deserve the way they treated you. It could lead to some closure and some self-awareness.

> (Example: Letter From My BF)
> I'm sorry I cheated on you.
> I'm sorry I allowed my body to speak for me,
> I promise I love you more.
> I'm sorry I asked you if those pants were yours,
> But they were actually hers.
> I'm sorry she caused your eating disorder,
> Her thin frame was not why I cheated,
> Your body was not why I cheated,
> You are perfect.
> I know when I'm driving,

And your gazing at the sun's sap lingering downward into your eyes,
 That I know you're thinking of her and I.
 I know you're wondering what happened the night I escaped,
 Got too drunk,
 And let it intoxicate me.
 I'm sorry you found us laying in my bed,
 Half naked,
 I'm sorry I let her wear your pajamas.
 Wear your shirt.
 I'm sorry you can never wear those clothes again.
 For they remind you of my mistake.
 I'm sorry I cheated on you.
 I'm sorry you love me too much to let go,
 Let go of the pain I have caused for two years of your life,
 I'm sorry you'll never forget about me,
 That I am always in the back of your mind, wandering,
 I'm sorry I don't feel as much love for you anymore.
 I'm sorry I haven't told you this,
 But my actions speak louder than words.
 I'm sorry.

49. REMEMBER TO BREATHE

Here's a good one that individuals have a hard time with... breathe! Your lungs begin to pinch, shriveling up like raisins. They squeeze, pull, and tear, and you feel as though you may be dying! This is probably an anxiety attack. But, don't be afraid! Breathing is the key to combating any anxiety attack. Through your nose, out your mouth, try this breathing exercise! While doing it, think of things in the present in which you can smell, such as fresh roses blooming, grass with sap dripping down the sides, and inhale that scent.

Throughout my high school years, it would have been incredibly beneficial if I took the time to breathe. Like before a big assignment, or a class presentation, letting myself become mindful of my lungs and heart, and how even after what I am doing, everything will still be there, helps me get centered, and in the right mind to practice mindfulness.

It sounds irrelevant since the main component to survive life is breathing, but when we actually take time out of the day to sit down and be aware of our breath, it does wonders. Feel the way your chest rises and falls. Feel your lungs filling with oxygen, and exhaling carbon dioxide. You can even practice a five by five breathing technique:

1. Inhale for five seconds.
2. Exhale for five seconds.

3. Repeat five times, each time breathing in one second less. (After 5 seconds, go down for four, after four, go down to three, etc.)

Breathing is a great mindfulness activity to bring us back to the present. After reading this, you may want to take some time to focus on your breathing!

50. MOMENT OF SILENCE

After all my tips, tricks, and facts, I would like anyone reading to take a moment of silence. Away from your phone, away from distractions, and sit silent. Take a moment of this silence for yourself, for anyone still in recovery, for the individuals not ready to take the steps towards healing, and for those in traumatic environment still.

I really appreciate you taking the time and I hope all of this gave you a little more background on what the disorder is. Keep breathing and stay strong! You got this.

To Summarize...

To summarize, Post Traumatic Stress Disorder is a real mental illness, that affects many individuals throughout the world everyday. From the people at your local Target, to even your best friend. PTSD does not discriminate, therefore the survivor can be anyone, anywhere. Be mindful what you bring up to just about anyone, for if it is related to their experience, they may get triggered. Attempt to close doors softly, step quietly in hospitals, and lower your voice indoors. This all can be great ways to reduce the risk of triggering someone.

If you feel like you are being affected by PTSD, I want to say I am sorry for whatever you may have went through. No one deserves PTSD to happen to them, for it is a lifelong struggle of taking control back from your abuser/event that caused you stress. There is no road map, but I do suggest starting somewhere small. Beginning to find a therapist in your network, can be scary, but unraveling everything that happened in a safe environment is the best next right step towards recovery. Support groups are there at your fingertips to aid you in the awareness of your disorder. You are not alone in this, it may seem like internalizing your pain is okay, but it will only lead to further self destruction. Keeping it a secret is definitely not good, so when you are ready, at your own timeline and speed, make the phone call. It will only benefit you.

For those reading to be more aware of the disorder, congratulations! You have successfully been a great being for learning more about a mental illness. Mental illness is so misunderstood to so many. The stigmas that arise from this disorder are countless. No one deserves to go through rough patches in life, but they do mold who we are and who we will be in the future, therefore mental illness that stems from trauma, is valid and real. Please share if you found this article at all helpful, for it may help someone else in distress as well. Thank you for taking the time to read this, wish you all luck in the future.

READ OTHER 50 THINGS TO KNOW BOOKS

50 Things to Know to Get Things Done Fast: Easy Tips for Success

50 Things to Know About Going Green: Simple Changes to Start Today

50 Things to Know to Live a Happy Life Series

50 Things to Know to Organize Your Life: A Quick Start Guide to Declutter, Organize, and Live Simply

50 Things to Know About Being a Minimalist: Downsize, Organize, and Live Your Life

50 Things to Know About Speed Cleaning: How to Tidy Your Home in Minutes

50 Things to Know About Choosing the Right Path in Life

50 Things to Know to Get Rid of Clutter in Your Life: Evaluate, Purge, and Enjoy Living

50 Things to Know About Journal Writing: Exploring Your Innermost Thoughts & Feelings

50 Things to Know

Website: 50thingstoknow.com

Facebook: facebook.com/50thingstoknow

Pinterest: pinterest.com/lbrennec

YouTube: youtube.com/user/50ThingsToKnow

Twitter: twitter.com/50ttk

Mailing List: Join the 50 Things to Know Mailing List to Learn About New Releases

50 Things to Know

Please leave your honest review of this book on Amazon and Goodreads. We appreciate your positive and constructive feedback. Thank you.

Printed in Great Britain
by Amazon